I0434522

Wisdom of The Ancestors

Wisdom of The Ancestors

Francis Mark-Maye

iUniverse, Inc.
New York Lincoln Shanghai

Wisdom of The Ancestors

All Rights Reserved © 2003 by Frank McMaye

No part of this book may be reproduced or transmitted in any form or by any means, graphic, electronic, or mechanical, including photocopying, recording, taping, or by any information storage retrieval system, without the written permission of the publisher.

iUniverse, Inc.

For information address:
iUniverse, Inc.
2021 Pine Lake Road, Suite 100
Lincoln, NE 68512
www.iuniverse.com

ISBN: 0-595-27272-X

Printed in the United States of America

To the memory of my father
Mark Maye Anabraba

The greatest man never known

And the women in my life:

Callie, Katie and Meg

Contents

PREFACE. xi

INTRODUCTION xiii

ANGER 1

BEAUTY 3

CAUTION. 5

CHARACTER 12

CHILDREN. 17

COMMUNITY 23

CONFIDENCE. 29

CONTENTMENT 31

COURAGE 34

DESTINY. 38

ENCOURAGEMENT. 41

EXCELLENCE 43

FAITH 45

FAMILY. 46

FORGIVENESS. 50

GRATITUDE 53

GREED 56

HONESTY 59

HOPE 61

HUMILITY 64

INTELLIGENCE 70

JUSTICE 75

KINDNESS 78

KNOWLEDGE 80

LAZINESS 85

LOVE 87

MARRIAGE 88

MODERATION 96

PARENTS 101

PATIENCE 104

PROGRESS 105

REALITY 106

RELATIONSHIP 112

RESPECT 113

RESPONSIBILITY 116

SELF RELIANCE 120

TRUST 122

UNDERSTANDING 124

VALUES 127

VANITY 130

WEALTH 131

WISDOM 134

PREFACE

Most cultures in the world make use of proverbs, defined as "a short, pithy saying in frequent and widespread use, expressing a well-known truth or fact (New Heritage)." Proverbs are a means to educate community members about the wiser ways of living, to heal emotional wounds, and also to subtly chastise when one has gone astray. They have most often been told by elders to the young, who from an early age, learn to interpret and make use of the metaphors; a skill observed as quickly dying in the post-modern West.

It is the metaphor, "a figure of speech in which a term is transferred from the object it ordinarily represents to an object it may designate only by implicit comparison or analogy (New Heritage)," that is noteworthy. Its abundant use is clear in the literature and music of Africa, Asia, and the Mid-East, yet increasingly lacking in the West. To understand metaphor, one must be comfortable with ambiguity and abstraction, observant of commonalities between self and other species and entities—objects even, and be literary in scope. The ability to see how the cloud and the sky might represent the child and the father is crucial to understanding and using proverbs effectively. A recent syndicated sitcom was seen in which a conflict had arisen between a father and his 18 year old son. The father, in attempting to teach his son appropriate conduct on the job announced, "There's an old saying…Don't fish off the company pier." To which his son replied, "Dad, I don't even work at a pier, I work at the video store!" While a humorous, media example of the increasing inability of youths of this culture to understand and make use of metaphor, it illustrates a significant change in our culture which insists upon realism at all costs and hinders our ability, or patience, to manipulate more abstract information.

The African people throughout the Continent have elevated the proverb to an art form, a therapy, a teaching tool. The proverbs presented in this book represent but a fraction of those that actually exist and are in use every day, even still. The ability to communicate in subtleties is not lost on the African people—it is a cultural tradition and etiquette, and often a necessity. We hope that you find the proverbs in this book useful. We hope that you find ways to introduce them in your life as teaching and healing tools. It is the resurrection of the use of proverbs in modern culture that will keep us firmly rooted to our history and connected implicitly to all things.

Dr. Stephanie McKyver Etukudo

Santa Clara University

INTRODUCTION

My dad always told me: "A true son of the soil, no matter in what culture, does not need too many words to understand something or express his point of view." As a kid growing up in a culture of few words and several meanings I often wondered about several things. It was not unusual to hear an elder mutter a single word and get everyone laughing riotously. I saw a man explode into a fury of anger because another man walking by made some subtle gesture, which meant an insult. All I saw was a man wearing a smile and looking down at his own feet as he shuffled by. As I grew up I began to understand some of the sayings of the elders but not everything.

"How come old people speak a different language?" I asked my dad once.

"It's the same language, son", he had laughed.

"Then how can I understand all of it? They sound so different"

"If you just understand the few that you hear, and use them, you will not need to understand all of them. No one does."

Apparently he noticed that I was not quite satisfied with his answer. He smiled at me and added.

"You younger generations have an advantage that we did not have: you can read and write. If I was you, I would write down every wise saying that I hear, and create a collection; instead of trying to remember all of them."

We spent hours talking that day. At the conclusion he gave me this last advice,

"Also, talk to your grandmother, and the other elders. Every individual, every language group and culture, have their own way of saying the same things."

"You must promise to share what I tell you with all your brothers and sisters. It belongs to them too", he added thoughtfully.

I remember being so excited I promised, not only to share it with my brothers and sisters, but friends and anyone interested in just a little more understanding of life. If you find any part of these writing beneficial to you, I will have kept my promise.

Compiling these sayings turned out to be more difficult than I had anticipated. Some of these proverbs exist in most cultures in one form or another and some times the interpretations vary. The challenge I faced was to try to provide enough clues to some of the more regional proverbs for my readers to get a hint of a meaning, without restricting them to one particular interpretation-mine. As a compromise I have added annotations to each proverb to explain a usage of the particular proverb and the source as I have heard them used. Those proverbs that I found more common among several cultures in their interpretations and usage, I have attributed to "The Ancestors" Whether you use them as explained or adopt them to your particular understanding, I hope they are of some value to you and your family.

In writing this book, I am greatly indebted to several people especially to members of the *African Education and Research Foundation* who were a constant source of inspiration, motivation and support for this project.

ANGER

- **Don't forget to revoke a curse that you had invoked in time of anger. A loose curse will eventually float back to its source.**

 —The Ancestors

We say things we don't mean in times of anger, if we don't recall what is said and apologize, we could be taken seriously and dealt with accordingly.

- **Don't send a hot-tempered man to war. He'll die before the war begins.**

 —The Ancestors

Anger will destroy an otherwise perfect plan.

- **The mosquito says, don't take offense because he buzzes in your ears. For what he knows about you sleeping with your clothes off, is best whispered directly into your ears.**

—Ijaw proverb

If we are patient, we'll notice that even the most annoying things have a purpose.

BEAUTY

- **A beautiful woman is like "Asukwo" palm fruit: smooth skin, all flesh and no bones.**

  —Ibibio proverb.

  Good palm fruits are smooth and fleshy in texture. (Ibibio is a tribe of Eastern Nigeria)

- **Only fools underestimate the power of a woman's bottom.**

  —Nigerian proverb

  A beautiful woman can exercise undue influence over a man.

- **The walking of a graceful woman is better than her dancing.**

  —Nembe proverb.

  A graceful walk is the sign of elegance in a woman. (Nembe is a sub-tribe of the Ijaw tribe in Southern Nigeria.)

- **A beautiful woman is like perfume. You don't want to wash your hands after you have touched her.**

  —kalabari proverb.

  The memory of being with a beautiful woman lasts for a long time. [Kalabari is a small language group that lives in city-states in the delta region of southern Nigeria.]

CAUTION

- **The toad does not jump onto the road in daylight for no reason.**

  —**Ibo proverb**

  There is always a reason for everything that happens. [Ibo is a large tribe that occupies most of the former Eastern Nigeria in Africa].

- **You can spit on an old man because you know what he is. But don't spit on a young man for you don't know what he'll become.**

  —**Ibo proverb**

  Don't be hurtful and mean to people, especially people you don't know very well.

• **The wild cat is not interested in eating the first little rat he catches. He only wants it to cry so he could find the mother.**
                                        —Ashanti proverb

Don't react immediately to everything that happens before you know the underlying reason. You can walk into a bigger trouble. (The Ashanti are a large tribe in Ghana with substantial historical significance.)

• *Egbe*, **the bird, says he always stands on one leg-just in case.**
                                        —Kalabari proverb

Things are not always as promising as they seem.
[Egbe is a long legged fishing bird that stands on one leg when it rested on the shores, which are some times not as firm as they look from a distance].

- **If your enemy suddenly disappears from the battlefield, run home to see about your women and children.**

  —**Benin proverb**

  Watch out for people who don't like you but suddenly show affection towards you. They may still be trying to hurt you where you least suspect. [Benin is a large tribe in the former Midwestern Nigeria, but this proverb is from the country of Benin in West Africa and formerly called Dahomey.]

- **Who gets trampled to death by an elephant had to be deaf.**

  —**The Ancestors**

  Disaster usually follows several warnings that were ignored. [The elephant can't move through the bushes without making a lot of noise.]

- **Anyone who is impressed with your front appearance but still wants to inspect your back also is looking for your weakness.**

—**Kalabari proverb**

Some people may congratulate you openly on your achievements, but behind you they wonder if you have fairly earned what you have.

- **If you don't want a stick to prick you in the eye, you must notice it while it is far and call out a warning.**

—**Oro proverb**

If you suspect that someone or something may hurt you in the future, take preventive steps now. [Oro is a group of villages speaking a dialect of Yoruba in Kwara State of Nigeria]

- **Don't be too sweet, people will leak you up.**

  —**Okirika proverb**

  If you always try to please people, they'll use you.
  [Okirika is a small language group that lives in city-states in the delta region of southern Nigeria.]

- **When the handshake goes beyond the elbow, it becomes a challenge.**

  —**Kalabari proverb**

  With friendly gestures, someone may actually be sizing you up to know your strength. You should learn the difference.

- **Dancing with a tiger, is tongue and teeth**

     —**Kalabari proverb**

     When dealing with a powerful person, know that it is a balancing act; Whatever goes wrong is always to your disadvantage

- **The snail says it marks its trail, in case it has to return home in the dark.**

     —**Kalabari proverb**

     It is good to be prepared for all possibilities when engaging in an endeavor.

- **For Play, for play, you are calling me names**

—Kalabari proverb

You claim that you are just joking with me, but in fact your are making damaging remarks about me.

CHARACTER

- Let the cow keep himself in good condition: If the horn is good we will drink from it; If the tail is good we will dance with it.

  —Ibo proverb

  A habit of good character will ultimately lead to responsibility, honor and respect.

- A servant who behaves himself like a son could have his master's name some day. A son who conducts himself like a servant will some day become one.

  —The Ancestors

  People will treat you according to the way you conduct yourself.

- **If you are born right, you will hear the drums without effort.**

  —Yoruba proverb

A proper up-bringing, makes it easier to understand true meanings of events and behaviors of people.

- **Better to be a common man and have the mournful flute played at your funeral, than be a king whose death is marked by the dance drum.**

  —The Ancestors

Being likeable is preferred over being mean even if you are powerful.

- **Foreigners make the most noise.**

—**The Ancestors**

A 'foreigner' represents a novice to a trade or art form, who doesn't quite yet understand the subtleties of it. He is most likely to boast about what he can do.

- **When you behave yourself so that no one can ask you: "Who are you?" you know you have succeeded.**

—**The Ancestors**

"Who are you?" means you are nobody; not recognized. It could also mean "Whose offspring. are you?" meaning your ancestry (or accomplishment) is not so distinguished that you should be so proud. With a good character, no one needs to ask the question.

- **The drums will recognize your ancestry from the manner in which you walk across the dance arena.**

  —Edo proverb

  You don't need to impress people with who you think you are; they'll know from the way you carry yourself. [Edo is a tribe of the former Midwestern Region of Nigeria. It is also the name of state occupied by this tribe in Nigeria].

- **The only way a woman can climb on a tall tree, is if it falls down.**

  —The Ancestors

  You will not be disrespected unless you put yourself in the position to be.

- **A child that washes his hands clean can eat with kings.**

—**Ibo proverb**

If you act responsibly, you will be rewarded with higher respect

- **Don't observe your reflection in the lake for too long. You may love it and want to embrace it, or hate it and want to fight it. Either way, you'll fall into the lake and get wet.**

—**The Ancestors.**

Vanity always comes with a price.

CHILDREN

- **A child who raises his voice against his parents has lost the right to defend them when his peers insult them.**

  —The Ancestors

  Your friends will think it's okay to insult your parents if they see you do it.

- **A good child has several mothers, but even the true mother of a bad child is ashamed to admit publicly.**

  —The Ancestors

  A well-behaved child will be protected. [In a village setting any woman old enough to be your mother can act on her behalf to prevent you from being beaten up by bigger kids]

- **Don't spread rumors the source of which you don't know, you could be exposing your mother's secret.**

                                            —The Ancestors

If you expose others weaknesses they will expose yours.

- **Fighting among brothers brings tears to the eyes of the Ancestors.**

                                            —The Ancestors

It is believed that the ancestors are always protecting their living descendants. When two brothers fight,they can't take sides. Practically, 'Ancestors' represents parents and relatives who can only be saddened by family quarrels since they can't take sides.

- **A branch that tries to be bigger than the tree will break off and fall to the ground.**

                                                    —The Ancestors

    If you despise, or ignore your family, they'll not support you when you need them.

- **Don't make your mother cry and curse you while holding her stomach from which you came. That curse is forever and you'll never amount to anything in life.**

                                                    —The Ancestors

    When a mother holds her stomach she is calling the debt her child owes her for the life she gave it. And that debt can never be repaid; it can only be forgiven. A child who causes a mother to call the debt cannot use its life since it cannot pay for the life.

- **He who cheats a child, cheats his God**

—**Kalabari proverb**

Don't expect to get away with cheating the defenseless. God defends the innocent.

- **A child who starts drinking wine at an early age, will grow up to become the village fool.**

—**Fulani proverb**

Early drinking is habit forming. [Fulani is a tribe in former Northern Nigeria]

- **Be always thankful to your mother, she could have killed you before you were born.**

  —The Ancestors

  Not all women want children. A child should be grateful his mother chose to have him.

- **A stupid child is like a boat on land. Wherever you push it to, that's where it stays until you push it again.**

  —The Ancestors

  Smart kids don't need step-by-step instruction to get a job done.

- **She who doesn't have a child becomes the witch.**

  —**Kalabari proverb**

  A woman with no child is always wrongfully suspected of wishing evil for other people's children.

- **A rude child is like a fly. A fly will perch on the nose of anyone, even of kings.**

  —**Kalabari proverb**

  A woman with no child is always wrongfully suspected of wishing evil for other people's children.

COMMUNITY

- **The blood of a true son of the soil must never touch the ground.**

  —The Ancestors

  A 'true son' is one who loves his community. The community will also protect him.

- **The rainbow is the sign of the peace agreement between the rain and the sun. Whenever you see it, remember to make peace for you are not bigger than the sun or the rain.**

  —The Ancestors

  It takes humility to admit your faults, and everyone needs to do that to live in peace.

- **The gods don't kill until men summon them to.**

> —The Ancestors

When people are hateful, rather than help someone in trouble, they'll help to destroy him and then say he was unlucky.

- **Ajuko is not a god. He is the spirit blamed when the youth of the land set about destroying the land. And that is shameful.**

> —Kalabari proverb

It is shameful to destroy things and not be brave enough to claim responsibility. [Ajuko is the name of a god in Kalabari culture that apparently destroys farms and houses without any reason.]

- No matter how rich you are, you cannot buy *Gbasah*, the drum title. It is not how much a man gets from society but by how much he gives to society that earns a man a *Gbasah*!

  —Kalabari proverb

"Gbasah means protector, or a huge tree that provides shades. It is the highest citizen honor in Kalabari land. It used to be given to brave men who would risk their lives to defend a village.

- "Give me a little, don't eat alone" is how three brothers became a nation.

  —Ijaw proverb

Sharing has a synergistic effect that helps communities to grow

- **Don't toilet on public playground, your children will step in it and bring it home.**

    —The Ancestors

    When you destroy public property, you deny other people's children as well yours.

- **"I saw your boat floating away," is no consolation to me.**

    —The Ancestors

    If you saw something bad happening to me but didn't move to help me, it doesn't do me any good that you saw it happen.

- **If any friend runs to you to tell you he overheard someone insulting you behind your back, ask him if he spoke up on your behalf. If he didn't, he is only stirring up trouble between you and another. He is not a good friend.**

—The Ancestors

Don't act on hearsay

- **Whoever keeps for himself what belongs to the community shames his ancestors who died for it.**

—The Ancestors

True spirit of community is sharing

- **He who doesn't know the town, will walk upon a grave and not know it.**

—Ijaw Proverb

Be careful when you are in a new environment, you can violate some very important community rules without meaning to.

CONFIDENCE

- **If a man firmly says, 'Yes', his God will say 'Yes'.**

  —The Ancestors

Man controls his fate.

- **The vulture is not patient without a reason**

  —The Ancestors

The vulture is sure that sooner or later, something will die for it to eat. People who are known for their meanness don't suddenly turn generous for no reason.

- **"The roar of the lion, doesn't wake me up", says the shark.**

  —Ijaw proverb

  Concentrate on your own strength, and you won't have to be intimidated by someone else's abilities. [The shark is as much a king in the sea, as is the lion on land.]

- **"I'm sleeping here, move the road", says the Sikaka tree.**

  —Ijaw proverb

  Used to describe dominating or intimidating people or circumstances. [Sikaka is a breed of iroko tree that grows in the rain forest to very great size. Some times it would fall across a main thoroughfare, and there's nothing travelers can do immediately except find a way around it].

CONTENTMENT

- As the Rooster would say to the Eagle, "Who needs to fly high when I can walk among men; two feet to two feet?"

  —The Ancestors

You may not be what others expected of you-have wings but can't fly. But there is something honorable about whatever you become.

- "I am tired" is not "I am lazy"

  —Nigerian proverb

Don't wear yourself down to impress others. Be contented to with your achievements and rest when you need to.

- **He whom the whole world rejects, does he reject himself too?**

  —Ibo proverb

People may think you are worthless, but you are worth something to yourself.

- **Don't envy a man because he is on top of the tree; you don't know if he is stuck there and can't come down.**

  —The Ancestors

Don't envy anyone simply by his appearance.

- **I don't have a problem with you until you let your problem begin to mix with my problem.**

  —The Ancestors

  Most people won't bother you until you begin to inconvenience them.

- **The alligator left the river for the land hoping for a better life, but ended up in the house that the turtle had abandoned and gone into the river seeking a better life.**

  —The Ancestors

  Don't throw away what you have to go after what someone else has. No one is ever completely satisfied.

COURAGE

- "Ask me what I know: Time to crow. Don't ask me what I don't know: Time to die. A real man must crow every morning with no regard for the day of death", says the Rooster.

  —The Ancestors

  Don't let fear prevent you from having a full life and doing what you are want to do (Roosters are frequently killed to serve as meat during festivals while hens are bred to lay eggs.)

- A great spirit was once a man who was brave enough to challenge a spirit to a wrestling match and won.

  —The Ancestors

  Overcoming your fears is the key to greatness

• **He who encounters the enemy first, is the Lion of the town.**

　　　　　　　　　　　　　　　　　—**Zulu Proverb**

> Even if you've always thought of yourself as weak, or incapable, you may some day find yourself in a position where a lot of people depend on you. You will have to be brave for their sake.

• **A curse is not happy when you are standing still.**

　　　　　　　　　　　　　　　　　—**Kalabari proverb**

> It you are not afraid and decide to ignore people's bad wishes for you, they will become ineffective.

- **Only those who are brave enough to hunt in the forbidden forest can tell the forbidden stories.**

  —**The Ancestors**

  You must do what most people cannot do, to get what most people cannot get. (A forbidden forest is usually full of wild animals. It is forbidden because most people don't come back from it.)

- **A man should die before giving up his guests to be killed.**

  —**The Ancestors**

  It is considered cowardly to let anyone capture your guests. Their pursuers must wait outside until the guest surrenders voluntarily.

- **A death not heard by the ear, doesn't kill.**

  —Kalabari proverb

  No matter how bad a threat is, we are not afraid of it until we hear it.

- **The ant was asked "Why do you challenge the elephant, knowing it will climb on you just once and you'll be dead?" "Not if I climb on him first", the ant replied.**

  —Ibo Proverb

  With courage and careful study of situations, there is always a way to get around the most formidable challenges

DESTINY

- **Pride is the number one killer of Destiny**

—The Ancestors

A person gifted to accomplish great things, can lose it all because of pride.

- **The fate you signed up for while in Heaven, you can revoke here on earth**

—Kalabari Proverb

If life is not compromising with you, you can always change the direction of your life. You don't have to live with an unfavorable condition, because you believe it is your destiny.

- **Our Father gave me this: it is mine! Look for yours in our Father's box, not in my hand.**
                                                    —The Ancestors

    You don't need to envy anyone. Everyone has a special gift from God.

- **When a man's time is up, he will do the stupidest thing just to die.**
                                                    —The Ancestors

    Time to die cannot be postponed.

• **The Chicken pecks, takes a step to peck again. The eaglet pecks, takes a step and looks up in the sky**

—**Kalabari proverb**

Even at youth, our individual personalities are prominent.

• **Man has no say in what God is working on.**

—**Ijaw proverb**

What God has destined for a person, he will become, even if some powerful human being try to prevent it from happening. Therefore do be discouraged because of human threat.

ENCOURAGEMENT

- He who digs the pit and he who stands by and urges him on are both equally working.

  —The Ancestors

  Encouraging others is as valuable as doing the work yourself.

- If your house burns down to the ground, don't feel so bad; the termites that you have been trying kill are dead too.

  —The Ancestors

  There is always something positive in every disaster.

- **The bedbug told his children, "Be patient. Whatever is hot right now will eventually cool off."**

—The Ancestors

Don't be discouraged by tough times. They don't last forever.

- **"Failure" and "Try Again" never get along.**

—The Ancestors

As long as you keep on trying, failure has chance. [Persistence and failure cannot exist together].

EXCELLENCE

- **If you have to eat a toad, you should eat the fattest one. That way if anyone asks you if you are a 'toad-eater', you can stand up and proudly say, 'Yes, I am!'**

  —The Ancestors

Do the best in whatever you do, no matter what it is, even if it is not a socially popular endeavor

- **Little fishermen fish in the river to buy food for their children. Great fishermen fish in the ocean to become 'Payree.'**

  —The Ancestors

Pursuit of excellence demands motivation beyond minimum requirement to get the job done. ('Payree' is the title given to someone who catches a great shark, or kills a lion.)

- Accused of being arrogant, the kite replied, "I don't fly so high to show off, but to show my children down there, how high they too can go."

—Hausa proverb

Pursuit if excellence is not arrogance. It can show others what they too can achieve. (Hausa is a language group in Northern Nigeria.)

- The eagle told his children, "I can tear any prey to pieces with my claws alone; but I always use the beak also just to make sure."

—Edo proverb

Doing more than minimum requirement guarantees success.

FAITH

- **From the back of the cow without a tail, God drives the flies.**
  —**The Ancestors**

God helps the helpless.

- **He who God does not kill, cannot be killed by man.**
  —**Kalabari Proverb**

Human hatred cannot harm you if God is with you.

FAMILY

- **Look into the situation of your family before you name a child.**
  —**The Ancestors**

Don't encourage your children to portray what they are not.

- **Don't name your child according to the condition you are in, but according to the condition you want the child to be.**
  —**The Ancestors**

Let your children know they can achieve more than you have. (It is common to name children in form of statement reflecting the hopes, conditions or the history of the family.)

• **A brother is more important than a friend; at the time of death, it will be your brother who gets called.**

—The Ancestors

Don't betray you blood relatives to an outsider. (Burial rites are performed only by blood relatives.)

• **Who will ever admit that his mother's soup doesn't taste the best.**

—The Ancestors

Everyone thinks his mom is the greatest mom

- **The secret of the mouth is known to the chewing stick, the secret of the trees is known to the monkeys, the secret of the road is known to the hunters who ply it. May our secrets be known only to us.**

  —Yoruba proverb

  Every family has a secret, you don't need to publicize yours.

- **Don't sell out your family's weakness for a stranger's laughter**

  —Kalabari proverb

  Don't expose your personal life to ridicule just to get the approval and acceptance of an outsider.

- **The mother's helper, and the town-walker, whose womb carries a family?**

  —The Ancestors

  A young girl who stays home and helps her mother, is more likely to get married and raise a family. A 'town-walker' is the same as a streetwalker.

- **The whispering bird, nests alone.**

  —The Ancestors

  Gossip among relatives can pitch them against each other and ultimately alienate the gossiper.

FORGIVENESS

- **If insults could kill, all the monkeys would be dead.**
  —The Ancestors

Don't pay attentions to verbal insults from ignorant people. The cannot harm you.

- **Please go with it; there's a bigger boat waiting for you downstream.**
  —The Ancestors

I'd rather not fight with you; sooner or later you will run into someone who is more willing and capable to deal with you.

- **Don't threaten to kill any man; you don't know his day.**

  —kalabari proverb

  You don't know when any man is destined to die. If you threaten him and he dies soon after, you'll be accused of killing him even if you didn't do it.

- **If you have children, do not dig pits for other people. It may be your child that ultimately crawls into it.**

  —The Ancestors

  If you plan evil for other people, it may come back to hurt people you love.

- **Settle your differences before the gods settle them for you; you may not like their decision and you cannot argue.**

—**The Ancestors**

Make peace with your offender rather then engage in prolonged antagonistic relationship. You can't control how the end will eventually turn out.

GRATITUDE

- **You can be generous to a lame man, but don't expect him to change his walk for you.**

  —**The Ancestors**

  Don't be generous to people with the hope of changing their behavior in your favor.

- **Ungrateful people are like chicken; they eat and quickly wipe their beaks clean on the ground as though they never ate.**

  —**The Ancestors**

  The chickens and fowls are constantly wiping their beaks on the ground to keep them clean.

- **The dog always gets a hug because he first says thank you and then asks for the meat; the goat always gets a beating because he takes the meat, and says 'Naaah, is that all?**

  —**The Ancestors**

  Gratitude is always rewarded with appreciation, Ungratefulness often leads to being denied opportunities.

- **He who is carried on the back doesn't know how far the journey is.**

  —**The Ancestors**

  One without responsibility doesn't appreciate the effort.

- **If you remember God when you are in need, He will remember you when things get better.**

  —**The Ancestors**

  Always pay your vows.

- **The man who said "Thank you", has planted the seed of tomorrow's favor.**

  —**Kalabari proverb**

  Being grateful is the best way to get people to do a favor again in the future.

GREED

- Don't eat alone. Should pepper go down the wrong way, you will always have someone to fetch you a cup of water.

  —The Ancestors

Be charitable, others will return the favor.

- The fishing net is not made to capture crabs. It is the fate to die that drags the crabs into the net.

  —Ijaw proverb

Greed gets us in trouble.

- **He who eats what is left for the gods, will become food for the gods.**

  —The Ancestors

  If, out of greed, you consume things you don't know the source of, it could kill you.

- **"Come let's eat" is politeness not an invitation to the table.**

  —The Ancestors

  Don't take everything that's available, control yourself and say 'No, thank you' some times.

- **I asked you to accompany me to my in-law's house; why are you dressed up better than I?**

                —The Ancestors

> Know when someone is trying to undo you, even when they claim they are just being good friends. [Dressing well could be a way of attracting the friend's spouse].

HONESTY

- **The fish that was too big to bring home, belongs to the fisherman who was alone.**

  —The Ancestors

  When their egos are challenged, few people can stay honest.

- **A messenger who uses up what is entrusted to him to deliver, should just go and kill himself, and not return home.**

  —The Ancestors

  Betraying complete trust is the ultimate shame. (Messengers are the most trusted class of citizens in rural settings. A dishonest messenger is the ultimate embarrassment to his family-His family prefers him dead)

- **Little evils lead to witchcraft**

—Kalabari proverb

Being dishonest in little things, will ultimately cause one to commit bigger crimes.

HOPE

- **Don't kill yourself because the pigs rampaged your farm. They'll make a bonus meal out of you.**

  —The Ancestors

  When bad people destroy your efforts, don't quit; you make them even happier.

- **A bad harvest did not destroy the farm; the despair that let the weeds grow after the harvest is what destroyed the farm.**

  —Ogun proverb

  One bad result will not destroy you ability to succeed, but not doing anything at all will. (Ogun is a Yoruba subgroup and name of a state in western Nigeria)

• **Relax! God did not put your name on the problem.**

—**Ijaw proverb**

Be comforted. Problems are not personal and they'll not stay with you forever.

• **I have shot my arrow twice and each time I hit a log of wood, but know that I did not make my arrow for the wood.**

—**The Ancestors**

When your first few attempts fail, remember why you started in the first place, and keep on trying.

- **Perhaps it will be better tomorrow, is why the bat doesn't just let go and break his neck.**

  —Hausa Proverb

  If it is the hope for a better future that gives most people the strength to continue living (The bat sleeps head down. It were to let go, it would fall head first and break its neck.)

- **There is a God, is the poor man's prayer.**

  —West African proverb

  A rich man always has some plan to resolve his problem. The poor man who can't do anything about his problem always resorts to hope in Divine intervention.

HUMILITY

- He who is asking for something must be prepared to stretch his hands further out than he who is giving it.

  —Kalabari

  When you want something from someone, don't expect your benefactor to be as enthusiastic about giving it to you as you are about getting it. Be prepared to put up with some inconvenience.

- You own the yam, and you have the knife; what choice do I have but to take whatever you slice for me?

  —Ibo proverb

  Know when you have no leverage in a conflict or negotiation. Just take what is given you and go on.

• **The stubborn male goat grew beard because its owner grew beard. Comes the market day, we'll find out who really owns whom.**

—**Ibo Proverb**

Know your limitations, and don't challenge people who has the power to hurt you.[An owner will sell off a stubborn goat, even if the price is not right, just to get rid of it.]

• **Whatever has become too big for the land should enter the sea.**

—**Ijaw Proverb**

Don't push weak people around. If you are tough, prove it against people equally as tough as you. [The sea is believed to hold the biggest and toughest of creatures]

- **A Chief's son is not a chief.**

>   —**Kalabari proverb**

   Because your parents are highly respected doesn't mean you will automatically be. You must earn your own respect.

- **Remember, whenever you wear a whisker that you cannot defend, the cat will come after you. That's why the rat is never at peace.**

>   —**Kalabari proverb**

   When you claim to be something, people will expect you to perform.

- **If your own market is throwing you into debt, shouldn't you look
for another? There is no shame.**

  —**Ijaw proverb**

  When things become too expensive, instead of continu-
  ing to buy the things you are accustomed to, and get into
  debt as a result, look for less expensive alternatives. There
  is no shame in that.

- **You are not yet too big for the clan, until you have survived Suku
and the old lady.**

  —**Ikwerre proverb**

  No one is indispensable. [Suku was the long oracle of
  'Justice', of the Aro tribe of Eastern Nigeria. It was
  believed to be able to discern justice, and consume 'guilty'
  people. Usually young men never survived it. It was common practice that if an old woman accused a young man
  of murder, he would be sent to Suku to 'clear' himself,
  and in all probability he would not survive it. Communities used that to get rid of trouble-makers.

- **I am poor; I am like a hermit. Please don't step on me; I'll rather crawl into my hole.**

                                        —Ibibio proverb

I don't want to fight.

- **Don't bring me any troubles, you see I have no hair under my armpit.**

                                        —Yanagoa proverb

I can't afford any conflicts. [Hair in the armpit is a symbol of growing up, and being able to take care of yourself. It could also imply being able to fight your own battles of life] [Yanagoa is a tribe in Rivers State of Nigeria.]

- **What good is it to you that your forefathers could catch lions with bare hands if you can't catch a rabbit.**

—Benin proverb

Your parents' successes will not compensate for your personal failures.

- **Calculated living is not misery.**

—Kalabari proverb

It is wise to be frugal. That is not the same as being a miser or being cheap.

INTELLIGENCE

- **From the smell of the breath you can predict the content of the stomach.**

  —Edo proverb

It could mean that personalities develop early in children. Sometimes it is used to imply that little events should be used as warnings of more of the same to come.

- **God is on your side, doesn't mean you should climb a palm tree and let go.**

  —Ibo

Pray and then help yourself.

- It is true that good things could happen from your mistakes because others will learn from it. But you don't have to be the teacher of the whole village.

    —Hausa proverb

Make no excuses for your continuous failures.

- If you attend a feast where several cows were killed, but all you have in your bowl turns out to be a cow's rear parts, the host might be telling you something.

    —Efik proverb

Learn to understand unspoken messages.[Efik is a tribe in eastern Nigeria]

- **Don't believe a man who says he hasn't eaten for three days. By then he shouldn't be able to tell you he hasn't eaten for three days.**

  —Hausa proverb

Don't believe every sad story to get your sympathy.

- **If a friend shows up at your house every time you are ready to eat. Watch out! He might be saving his money to build a bigger house than you have.**

  —Yoruba proverb

Sharing what you have with people who are quite capable of taking care of themselves is not wise.

- **If you know you killed the lion's baby and the Lion is upset, what wisdom instructed you to hang the head of the baby lion on your front door?**

  —**Ashanti proverb**

  It is foolhardy to taunt someone who offended, especially if the person can harm you.

- **Don't tell the enemies the king has gone insane. Tie the king to the throne and rule land.**

  —**Benin proverb**

  Do not divulge your weakness unnecessarily; manage it instead and do your best.

- **The rat follows the lizard into the river, forgetting that when they come out, the lizard will be dry and but it won't be.**

—The Yanagoa

Don't copy other people, they may be equipped to get away with things that you can't.

- **Your finger in my face is not anger, it is "Who are you?"**

—Kalabari Proverb

When someone chooses violence or confrontation to settle a dispute between you and him, he is not just angry, he also thinks he can defeat you in a dual.

JUSTICE

- **Better to pay your debts on earth before you die; your creditor may have some wicked ancestors waiting for you out there after you die.**

  —The Ancestors

  Don't try to undo someone even if you can get away with it. Some how, you'll pay.

- **If you go shaking up a tough old bush, you're going to have some tough, old animals to deal with.**

  —The Ancestors

  If you start up a big confrontation, you'll attract very strong opposition.

- **He who secretly murders the innocent cannot hide it forever. In the end he will die with his face on the ground.**

 —**The Ancestors**

[It is believed in the Kalabari culture that evil people cannot die facing the light]

- **The hawk should perch and the eagle should perch. Whichever prevents the other from perching, may his wings break.**

 —**Ibo proverb**

There is room for everyone to succeed. Whoever prevents another from succeeding should himself fail.

- **The chicken never forgets who plucks his tail feathers during the raining season.**

  —**Kalabari proverb**

  People never forget who hurt them when they need help most. [The chicken needs its tail feathers to shield itself from the cold.]

- **If you didn't mind the taste of the hair when you bite someone's head, they will not mind the taste of the mucus when they bite your nose.**

  —**The Ancestors**

  If you have to go out of your way to hurt people, they will go to a lot of trouble just to hurt you back.

KINDNESS

• **Don't be mean to a stranger; he might be a spirit.**

—The Ancestors

Be kind to a stranger, he could be a blessing.

• **Compassion is not foolishness.**

—Kalabari proverb

Don't stop being compassionate to people because you are afraid others might consider you stupid or weak.

- **He who is doing good, has the gods and the ancestors at his service.**

  —The Ancestors

  Do good, it will return to you.

- **If you are eating and a dog is watching you and wagging its tail, what more proof do you need to acknowledge that it too wants some of the food; speak in a human tongue?**

  —Oro proverb

  Don't humiliate people who need your help. [Oyo is a dialect group among the Yoruba language.]

KNOWLEDGE

- He who dives into the sea looking for a way out, doesn't know where the door is."

  —Kalabari proverb

  Stop to think in times of crisis.

- Listening rather than talking is the mark of the true sons of the land, for that is how they are able to understand when the drum speaks.

  —The Ancestors

  You learn more from listening than from talking.

- Firmly secure anything of value in a boat. When a boat capsizes, the true treasures always run to the bottom of the sea. It is the garbage that floats on top.

  —Ijaw Proverb

  Value people who are important to you; people who don't care what you do are people you don't need.

- The sound of Ikiriko means it is time for celebration, but when you hear the Akuma sound, you know something of grave importance has happened. A man who left home and never returned may have confused the two.

  —Kalabari proverb

  Ignorance of your culture can get you trouble.

• **Ignorance is a disease that passes the skills of the witch doctors.**

—The Ancestors

You can't help an ignorant person.

• **Mushroom that normally grows on the ground, when it wants to deceive, goes and grows on the anthill.**

—Ibo proverb

Don't judge things by appearance only.

- **Don't teach a foolish man how to use the chewing stick; he'll chew up the entire bush.**

                                        —Ibo proverb

> Don't give a foolish man something valuable, he'll abuse it.

- **Good tongue is what the snail uses to overcome all obstructions.**

                                        —The Ancestors

> With good words you can talk yourself out of any trouble or difficulty.

- **Word is like a raw egg: once you drop it, you can't pick it back up.**
                                                                —The Ancestors

Be careful what you say; you can't withdraw it.

LAZINESS

- **If you rest your oars and let the tide take you where it wants, you can't complain when it tangles you up with a mangrove tree.**

  —Ijaw proverb

If you don't act, you'll have to settle for whatever you get.

- **Delay, delay, night has arrived.**

  —The Ancestors

Lazy person postpones things until his life is over.

- **Next day, next day, is laziness.**

—**The Ancestors**

Procrastination comes from laziness.

- **The goat that lies down, lies on his own skin mat.**

—**Ibo proverb**

Laziness can only hurt you and no one else. [Goat skin is used as mat to lie down and relax. A lazy goat is essentially skinning itself.].

LOVE

- **My dear, all the great love you have for me, is escaping through the bottom of the jewelry box.**

  —Kalabari Proverb

If you really love me, my jewelry box should be full, but the box is empty instead. A sarcastic way of saying you don't buy me things to show how much you say you love me. In a broader sense it could be used to imply that the words and the actions don't match.

MARRIAGE

- A bad marriage is like sewage water: You can't drink it, and you can't pour it out of the door. Either way it will stink. So you must cover it up properly and live with it.

  —Ibo Proverb

  To avoid scandal, you may have to put up with bad marriage.

- The hunter who uses his gun to guard his door instead of using it for hunting, turns the pot of meat into stone.

  —Bauchi Proverb

  A jealous husband who hangs around his house to watch his wife cannot be out making a living for his family at the same time. The family will go hungry, since they can't eat stone.

- **"Don't forget that your biggest catch is already at home," says the fisherman's wife.**

  —Okirika proverb

  A fisherman is very happy when he catches a big fish. The wife is saying "I love you and I can make you happier than any fish you can catch, so don't worry even if things don't go well today."

  Used as a love good bye as the husband goes out to work in the morning.

- **A good home is where a brother and a sister live.**

  —Edo Proverb

  A successful marriage, is one in which the couple treat each other with the same love, respect, tolerance and sense of permanent relationship as a brother and a sister would.

- **The palm tree that bears the sweet palm wine, is too dirty to be planted in the middle of the courtyard for shades.**

—**Efik Proverb**

A hard working spouse may not have the time to always look good. If you want your spouse to always look good, then know that he or she may not have time to work hard as well.

- **I wouldn't have known that your pot-cover fits my pot better than it fits your, if you hadn't loaned me your pot-cover in the first place.**

—**Ijaw Proverb**

Be careful when let your spouse get too familiar with your friend, They may find out they are more compatible and you will end up losing your spouse

- **Any woman who looks at men straight in the eyes will not make a faithful wife.**

  —**Yoruba Proverb**

  A flirtatious wife will not be faithful to her husband.

- **Whoever is steering the boat should chew the tobacco after meal. Let the other wash the dishes.**

  —**Ijaw Proverb**

  If the woman is the sole provider for the family, the man should do the domestic chores.

  [Used to tease men who get comfortable with their wives earning more money than they do.]

- **One who cannot speak up in the bedroom, now wants to speak for the town council; who wants to listen?**

> A man who is perceived as being unduly influenced by his wife, or just weak, is disregarded by his fellow men when he tries to voice his opinion.
>
> Often used to tease, or humiliate a husband who is openly in love with his wife, or whose wife is considered rather bold and vocal in public.

- **If a couple is fighting and no one is calling for help, you know it is the husband that is getting the beating.**
  —Kalabari Proverb

> When a family apparently in trouble is not seeking assistance, they have a secret to hide.

- **Don't tell your wife's secret to other men: if it's bad, they'll despise you; if it's good, they'll want to find out for themselves.**

  —The Ancestors

  Divulging your wife's weaknesses to strangers will ultimately come back to haunt you.

- **If you don't like somebody beating your mother, don't beat your wife; she is some else's mother.**

  —The Ancestors

  Your children will turn against you if you abuse their mother.

- **Don't eat anything that will make your children ashamed of taking the garbage out the next morning.**

                                                —Hausa Proverb

  Don't get caught doing anything that would embarrassment your children.

  [Often used to advice parents who are contemplating cheating on their spouses, planning some socially unacceptable act]

- **A good husband is his wife's pillow. A woman married to a bad husband sleeps on wood.**

                                                —Yoruba Proverb

  A good husband is his wife's support.

- **Before you marry a man, find out how his father treated his mother.**
  —The Ancestors

Wife abuse is sometimes hereditary.

MODERATION

- **The particular leaf that the goat finds so irresistibly tasty is the very leaf it will die from.**

    —Ibo Proverb

Bad habits can kill.

- **If you wrestle your opponent to the ground and quickly let him go, he will respect you for the rest of his life. But if you pin him down for everyone to see, you have made him a life enemy.**

    —Ikwerre Proverb

Be generous in victory.

- **When a melody becomes too sweet it brings out the spirits to dance on the streets.**

  —Ogoni Proverb

  Excessive pleasure seeking could lead to glorifying association with dangerous elements.

- **What tastes so sweet going into the mouth, will be just as painful coming out when you go to the toilet.**

  —Ibo Proverb

  Everything has a price.

- **Not knowing too much was what saved the village of Elele, for if Didia had known he was not allowed to fight because he was a slave, he wouldn't have picked up the weapon and saved the village.**

  —**Ikwerre Proverb**

  Unnecessary negative details could poison your mind. [Ikwerre is a tribe in Rivers State of Nigeria that speaks language similar to Ibo]

- **The Elephant has drunken the water and broken the water pot; is the dry season gone forever?**

  —**Ibo Proverb**

  Don't be careless with valuable things you have because things happen to be going well now; the tough times will eventually come again when you will need them.

- **Tomorrow is pregnant: It could be a boy or a girl, who know?.**

  —The Ancestors

  No one knows what the future holds.

- **When a monkey's hand stays in the soup for too long, it begins to look like a human hand.**

  —The Ancestors

  Overdoing anything get people suspicious. Also used to imply that a situation has been overused and needs to change

- **Two much pleasure will reduce the size of a town**

  —The Ancestors

Too much pleasure makes you to let your guard down. That's when an enemy can hurt you. [In war times when a town is celebrating is when they can get attacked and half of the town killed off]

PARENTS

- The eye had seven children and the mouth had only one child. The eye just sat and watched all her seven children get into mischief and die one at a time. But the mouth talked, and talked and talked her only child into manhood.

  —The Ancestors

  Never get tired of talking to your children about good values. It will pay off when they grow up.

- Children; who is throwing theirs away?

  —Kalabari proverb

  When your child gets in trouble and other people recommend stiff punishment for the child, always ask if they would recommend the same punishment for their own children, under similar circumstances.

• **No matter how low the tides get, the mark of the water level can never be erased from the creek.**

—**Ijaw proverb**

Values instilled in children will always remain with them when they grow up.

• **Don't open up the stomach of a crocodile in the presence of a child; you don't know what will come out of it.**

—**Nembe proverb**

Watch what you say in front of children; you can poison their minds.

- If you make your children ask, "Where is he?" when they are young, they will make you ask, "Where are they?" when you get old.

  —The Ancestors

If you don't take responsibility for your children when they are young and need you, they will not care about you when you are old and need them.

- Help me flog my child, doesn't come from the heart

  —The Ancestors

No parent likes to see other people punish their child, even for the right reasons.

PATIENCE

- 'Be patient, whatever is hot right now, will eventually cool off', the bedbug told his children.

  —**Ibo proverb**

Tough times don't last forever.

PROGRESS

- **Little by little is forward movement.**

—Ibo proverb

Progress comes in small steps.

REALITY

- The chicken that was snatched from his mother by the evil hawk says he cries out not because he expects anyone to save him, but that the world will know what happened to him.

  —The Ancestors

There are certain situations you can't do anything about—except tell someone.

- The crayfish said it used to walk straight like all other fishes. It is the conditions of the world that forced it to bend.

  —The Ancestors

Circumstances can make someone become something he didn't purposely plan to be.

- **A bald man that goes outside without a hat shouldn't blame the birds for leaving their droppings on his head.**

  —The Ancestors

  If you take risks, be prepared for possible disappointments.

- **Some problems are like Tsetse fly sitting on a your nose. If you leave it alone it will suck your blood; if you try to kill it he could have a bloody nose.**

  —The Ancestors

  Some problems will put you in a no-win situation.

- **Asked why he has such a rough skin, the crocodile replied: "Come live in my neighborhood for one day and you'll find out."**

  —Yanagoa proverb

  Don't judge people until you have known their circumstances.

- **Thing are so bad even the mosquitoes have swam across to the other side of the river; they don't want to bite me anymore.**

  —Nembe proverb

  Used to exaggerate tough times.
  [Mosquitoes feed on human blood. If humans don't eat, they won't have any blood for mosquitoes to feed on, so the mosquitoes go looking for other means of survival]

- **When the masquerades start entering their tents backwards, you know the play is over.**

> —**Abua proverb**

Know when to quit.

- **As the jelly fish says, "If the water should leave you on the shore, the best you can do is play dead until it returns, and no one will notice."**

> —**The Ancestors**

It's not smart to fuss about conditions you can't change. [When a fish is left on the shore, people notice it and pick it up because it keeps jumping up and down]

- **If the sun is up and you are still waiting for the day to break, the gods have kept your sight.**

—The Ancestors

Know when circumstances have changed and accept it. Don't sit around hoping for your glorious past to return. [When the gods keep your eyes, you have become blind.]

- **When the black bird begins to sing outside the window of a sick person, prepare for the funeral because the spirit is gone.**

—Ashanti proverb

No when a struggle is over.

- **"What else can I do?" is how I survive.**

  —Kalabari proverb

  Implies resignation to circumstances. [Often used to as response to greeting like "How are you doing?". Synonymous to "Just getting by." or "Just managing."

RELATIONSHIP

• **Dog play is 'You fall for me, I fall for you.'**

—**The Ancestors**

Fun relationship is about give and take.

• **Every yam plant needs a support stick to stand on to blossom.**

—**Ibo proverb**

Everybody needs someone to lean on. [Yams have weak, creeping stems. Sticks are usually provided for them to climb and grow upwards]

RESPECT

- What you don't know is older than you. Respect it as you would your elders.

  —Zulu proverb

Don't despise things you don't understand.

- He who holds his ancestors in great esteem, makes himself the son of great men.

  —The Ancestors

Whatever you make of your parents is your heritage.

• **What man has rejected, the gods will not accept.**

—**The Ancestors**

What you think is not good enough for you, consider it not good enough for your superiors.

• **A child who raises his hand against his parents, has asked for a village beating.**

—**The Ancestors**

If you treat your parents disrespectfully, your neighbors can turn against you on their behalf. [In a village setting, strong men can discipline a child who gets physical with his parents.]

- **He who holds a great man in high esteem, will ultimately become great himself.**

  —The Ancestors

  People tend to try to become like the people they respect and admire

RESPONSIBILITY

• **If you want to live a different life style, it is your duty to disown yourself from your ancestors.**

—The Ancestors

Act in a manner that will bring honor to your family. Carrying the name that the ancestors worked hard to preserve comes with a certain responsibility.

• **When a child mistakes a grown man for a playmate, that man has waited too long to get married.**

—The Ancestors

Every man should take on the responsibilities of a grown man.

- **When men were men, women built the nations.**

—The Ancestors

Men fight and destroy nations, women get together and dance, and build nation.

- **Only he who is willing to wash the pot should eat the last yam.**

—The Ancestors

If you won't do the work, you'll not get the most reward.

- **The fowls are acting drunk because the hawk hasn't shown up yet.**
  —**Ibo proverb**

People act irresponsibly in the absence of authority.

- **If a child carrying a basket on his head, trips twice, people will ultimately identify the content of the basket he's carrying.**
  —**The Ancestors**

If you are in a position of responsibility, don't be careless. [The purpose of carrying the basket on your head is so that people will not know what's in it.]

• **Failure to deliver a message is a dog's errand.**

> **—Kalabari proverb**

People who are easily distracted from their goals are compare to dogs. Throw a bone to a dog, and it abandons its initial goal.

SELF RELIANCE

- You don't know how you were born, and you don't know how you will die. Don't be a fool and let other people decide how you will live.

  —The Ancestors

Stand up for what you believe.

- When the lizard survives a fall from a tree and there's no one to praise him, he praises itself.

  —The Ancestors

Be proud of yourself, even if others don't praise you.

- **"Let me see you off" is courtesy; I can still get home without it.**
  —Ibo proverb

  Note: Because someone felt obligated to be nice to you, doesn't mean you couldn't have done without it.

TRUST

- **Don't go to war with men you do not own. They'll desert you when things get tough.**

    —**Kalabari proverb**

Don't do anything serious with uncommitted people.

- **A man who exposes his secret source of information should just go and kill himself.**

    —**The Ancestors**

One who breaks a trust can never again be completely trusted.

- Holding on to a crab's leg is like holding on to nothing. One pull and the crab will let go of you and the leg.

  —The Ancestors

Don't count on promises of unreliable people.

- Trust is an earthen water pot; once broken, it can never be put together again as it originally was

  —The Ancestors

Don't count on promises of unreliable people.

UNDERSTANDING

- Asked why he has his eyes on top of his head instead of on the sides like other fishes, the mudskipper replied: "Other fishes haven't been through what I have been through."

—Ijaw proverb

You need to understand people's life to understand why they are they way you see them. [The mudskipper is fish common in the delta area. It has a big head with big bulging eyes.]

- If a little child keeps crying and pointing to one direction of the bushes, look carefully: If his daddy hasn't gone that way, his mama must have.

—Kalabari proverb

When events keep repeating themselves, there is an underlying cause.

- **God knew what he was doing when he created Iyala and gave him no legs.**

  —Nembe proverb

  Certain apparent deficiencies serve a good purpose. [Iyala was a mean, powerful cripple who could kill with his bare hands. Fortunately he had no legs to pursue his offenders.]

- **What happens to another happens to an iron tree.**

  —Kalabari proverb.

  It is impossible to understand exactly how others feel. [Iron tree is so strong, that people generally don't pay attention to the cut marks on it.]

- **Until you have faced the door with your two feet, don't make fun of a lame man**

  —**Ijaw Proverb**

  Don't make fun of people who had misfortune. Until you are dead, you can't be sure that it won't happen to you too. [Facing the door with two feet, means the person is dead]

- **The bad old axe saves the house**

  —**Kalabari proverb**

  Some times the people in your life who are not exciting and colorful, are the ones you will depend on in times of dire needs.

VALUES

- **The goat doesn't understand jeear, the dog doesn't hear 'oroh', and the rooster doesn't obey 'Saah'—That's why the gods don't understand 'Sisi' anymore**

  —Kalabari proverb

  No one observes cultural values anymore; that's why our prayers don't get answered. ['Sisi', means please in Kalabari language. Jeear, oroh, saah, are words used to mimic the sounds of animals]

- **The murderer doesn't have to go to Suku anymore. The thief gets to live among the people. One man is allowed to hold another down. The women haven't counted one but they are counting two. These forbidden things are what drove the founding deity into the big sea and left us with "Who are we?"**

  —Okirika proverb

  Decay of moral values has erased the people's identity.

- **A true son of the land never wastes his words.**

—**The Ancestors**

A well-brought up person doesn't speak carelessly.

- **He who speaks too fast will lie without meaning to.**

—**The Ancestors**

Watch what you say.

- **If someone runs to you and says, "I have entered your door", do you ever give that person up to their pursuers?**

  —**Kalabari proverb**

  It usually implies, "If one has a major responsibility to perform does one walk away from it?"–a reverse way of saying, "I have a major responsibility that I must perform".

  ["I have entered your door" means "I have run to you for protection". It was customary to refrain from pursuing anyone who has run to another person, usually an older person, and declared the expression. If the pursuers tries to catch the person anyway, they put the 'protector' in a position to have to defend the person under their protection.

- **Whoever keeps for himself what belongs to the community shames his ancestors who died for it.**

  —**The Ancestors.**

  Leaders who use their position to exploit the community, became embarrassment to those who genuinely serve the community, often at their own personal cost.

VANITY

- **Don't observe your reflection from the lake for too long. You may love it and want to embrace it, or hate it and want to fight it. Either way you'll fall into lake and get wet.**

  —The Ancestors

Don't think of your own values too much, you could hurt yourself in the illusion.

WEALTH

- **Plenty does not come from gathering plenty, but from gathering and not throwing away.**

—The Ancestors

You get rich by saving what you make.

- **Children are wealth.**

—The Ancestors

Children are blessings just like money.

- **He who wants a beautiful woman wants a wealth consumer.**

—**The Ancestors**

A fun name for a beautiful woman is 'Wealth eater' in Ibo language

- **A poor man is a little boy**

—**The Ancestors**

If you are not rich, people rarely take your comments seriously.

- **Wealth is not a personal property**

—The Ancestors

No one owns exclusive right to wealth. Anyone can become wealthy

- **You can't buy tomorrow with money**

—The Ancestors

No matter how rich you are, you can't get any more of the next day, than anyone else. The future equally belongs to everyone.

WISDOM

• **Until the sun shows up, it is not wise to curse the night.**

—Ijaw proverb

Don't denounce what you have with the hope that something better is coming along.

• **Listening is long life**

—Kalabari proverb

You are more aware of your surroundings when you are listening than when you are talking. You can hear danger from afar and get out of the way.

- **Let the wise man bargain, and the rich man pay**

  —Kalabari proverb

  In every endeavor different people have different strengths, and it is wise that each person does what the person is best at, for the benefit of the team.

I hope *Wisdom of the Ancestors* has brought you as much value and satisfaction as it has brought me. One of my older uncles who contributed immensely to my understanding by these phrases, as we talked until very late one night, remarked, "Sleep is not important right now. I have been carrying with me treasures of several generations before me. This is my chance to fulfill my duty of passing them on–to you!" In the same spirit, I hope I have passed them on to you and your family.

Furthermore, I know that all people have *wisdom* of their ancestors. I sincerely hope that this collection has triggered in you some of the wisdom of *your* own ancestors.

The Author.

0-595-27272-X

www.ingramcontent.com/pod-product-compliance
Lightning Source LLC
Chambersburg PA
CBHW061307280526
45784CB00002B/924